· MY · FIRST · LOOK · AT ·

Clothes

DK

DORLING KINDERSLEY
London • New York • Stuttgart

Getting dressed

Every morning I put on my clothes.

Today I am wearing purple dungarees
and a yellow sweat-shirt.

Underwear

When I get up I put on my underwear.

socks

tights

singlet

pants

Night clothes

I wear my pyjamas to bed.

nightdress

pyjamas

dressing gown

slippers

Cold day clothes

I wrap up in warm clothes on cold days.

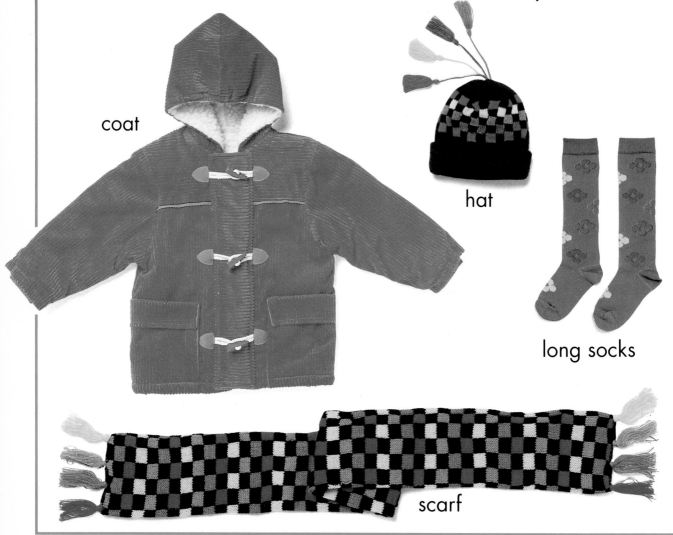

coat

hat

long socks

scarf

gloves

mittens

jumper

trousers

7

Hot day clothes

When it's hot, I wear clothes that keep me cool.

sunglasses

skirt

tee shirt

shorts

swimsuit

sunhat

sundress

Dressing-up clothes

It's fun to dress up in different outfits.

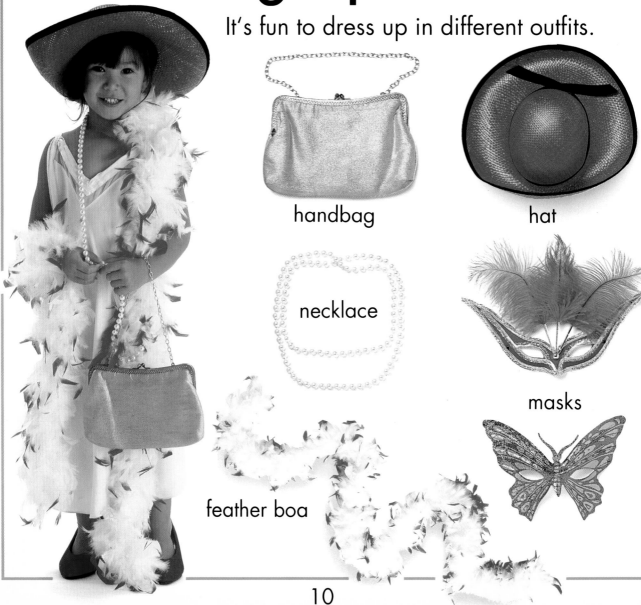

handbag

hat

necklace

masks

feather boa

10

party hats

scarf

sword

belt

eye patch

pirate's hat

beard

Sportswear

I wear special clothes to play different sports.

knee pads

shorts

cap

sneakers

tracksuit

socks

flippers

goggles

headbands

sports shirt

Shoes

I wear shoes to protect my feet.

party shoes

boots

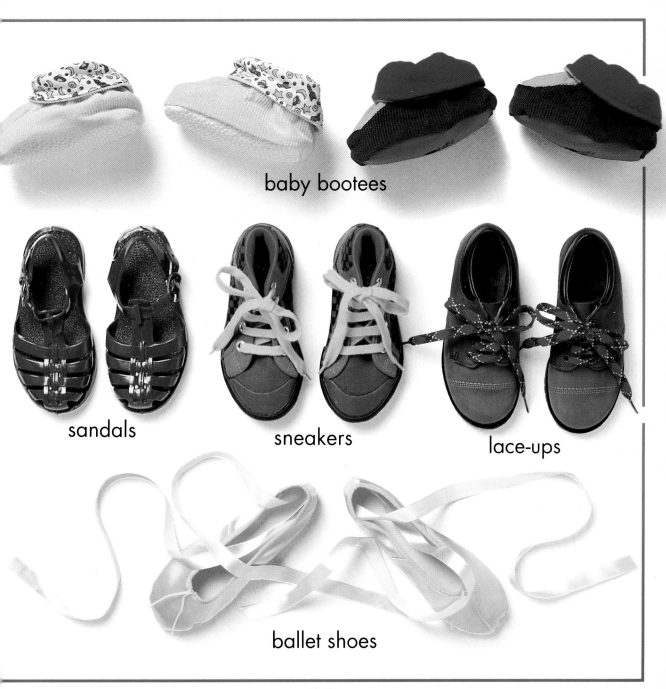

baby bootees

sandals

sneakers

lace-ups

ballet shoes

15

Hat puzzle

Here are six different hats. Do you know who wears each one?